T0095701

# WHAT'S THE DIFFERENCE?

## A Life with Disabilities but not a Disabled Life

## GARY GONDOS

iUniverse, Inc.
New York  Bloomington

# What's the Difference?

# A Life with Disabilities but not a Disabled Life

*iUniverse books may be ordered through booksellers or by contacting:*

*iUniverse*
*1663 Liberty Drive*
*Bloomington, IN 47403*
*www.iuniverse.com*
*1-800-Authors (1-800-288-4677)*

*Because of the dynamic nature of the Internet, any Web addresses or links contained in this book may have changed since publication and may no longer be valid. The views expressed in this work are solely those of the author and do not necessarily reflect the views of the publisher, and the publisher hereby disclaims any responsibility for them.*

*ISBN: 978-1-4502-5835-7 (sc)*
*ISBN: 978-1-4502-5836-4 (ebook)*

*Printed in the United States of America*

*iUniverse rev. date: 9/30/2010*

I would like to dedicate this book to my Brother, Brian. Our relationship has always been extremely close. He has always encouraged me to do anything and has always been there to help me accomplish my goals. Writing this book has been one of my goals and he was there all along the way to help me in my journey, remembering and recording the events that I have related. He has always been able to see ways for me to attack a task that perhaps others would seem daunting. He's a terrific teacher, brother, mentor and friend. I am extremely lucky to have such a wonderful brother.

# INTRODUCTION

You may have actually seen me.

I'm the person using a scooter whom you see going to work every day. I'm the person sitting in accessible seating at sporting events. I'm the person whom you might spot on the street who appears to have had a stroke.

Maybe you held the door for me. Or, maybe you politely stepped aside so that I could navigate my scooter through a crowd. Or, maybe just the sight of me led you to feel grateful that you are able-bodied.

Or, maybe you decided that it was simply too uncomfortable to acknowledge me.

Very likely, however, you did notice that I was different from you. You noticed that I had a disability. What else did you notice about me? To most people whom I encounter, my identity begins and ends with the fact that I, like many others, have a disability. Who I am, however, beyond my disability, is obscured by my being so "different."

Have you, in fact, seen *me*? Could you really know?

# CHAPTER 1

I think that many able-bodied people happen to believe that those who have disabilities are substantially different from them. Some people appear to believe that I do not want or expect to get the same things out of life that they do. Others seem to conclude that I am able to do very little independently.

But, that is not the case.

My disability may make me seem unlike others from the outside. Yet, I firmly believe that *I am much more similar to everyone else than I am different.*

*How much do outside appearances influence our opinions?*

Many people have misconceptions about how much I am "able" to do for myself. Even though it might take me a little longer, I manage to accomplish nearly all that I wish to do. I do not feel sorry for myself, nor do I wish others to feel sorry for me.

I wish I could somehow communicate this to people when they take their first glance at me. I would like to show that

I don't mind talking about my disability, and that I don't see my disability forming a big part of who I am. I would like to explain that despite my looking different, I really don't feel that much different from anyone else.

When I have been able to talk about my disability and my experiences, I have found that both the listener and I benefit. That has led me to write this book.

I'm 38 years old, and I live in an apartment in suburban Washington D.C. I have a job with the Federal Government. I enjoy spending time with family and friends. I look forward to one day having a family. That description of my life may not diverge much from a brief introduction to the lives of many other people close to my age. And, of course, that's the point. Yes, certain details may not be the same. My daily routine probably takes a little more time, thought and planning than the routines of many other people. But in the end, it's just a routine. The car that I drive needed several adaptations so that I could operate it, but I'm able to drive. I use a scooter most of the time to get around (I am able to walk short distances with a crutch) but I can go virtually anywhere I want.

I have worked hard to limit the impact that my disability has on my life. My greatest challenge, however, is one over which I feel I have the least power — specifically, getting others to realize that having a disability does not ultimately make me so much different from anyone else.

During a routine doctor's visit when I was five months old, the pediatrician noticed that I was in heart failure. My condition, later diagnosed as Total Anomalous Pulmonary Venous Return, was due to a malformation of my cardiac vessels. In short, my heart was not able to pump oxygenated blood to the rest of my body. Due to this condition, I urgently needed to undergo a procedure called a balloon septostomy which would temporarily improve my heart's functioning. The intervention was successful. Unfortunately, during the procedure, I suffered a stroke.

The stroke only affected the right side of my body, and I am told that I was able to nearly fully recover from this stroke with intensive daily physical therapy. At one point, I was even able to walk.

Then, when I was two-and-a-half years old, I needed to have a second surgery to permanently repair my heart defect. My family took me to Children's Hospital in Philadelphia for this procedure. My parents recall that the night before the surgery I was running around the hospital just as any young child might do.

The surgery was successful in that it repaired my heart defect. Unfortunately, though, I suffered another stroke. This more severe stroke was *bilateral* — both sides of my body were partially paralyzed, and it also affected my speech. (Unnoticed at that point, it had also caused learning disabilities.) Several days following this stroke, I was able to recover partial use of the left side of my body. I also started to regain some of my speech.

Soon after, I was released from the hospital. I returned home with my family and immediately started physical therapy. Being so young, I didn't really know why I was going to physical therapy. I recall being stretched out on a mat with little understanding of what was transpiring. At home, my parents carried me from room to room, or I slid around on the floor. When I went outside, I was pushed in a stroller. In addition to getting physical therapy, I worked with a speech therapist.

Gradually, with very intensive therapy, I was able to regain near-full functioning on my left side, though I remained with only extremely limited use of my right arm and leg.

And so it has been to this day.

# CHAPTER 2

The predominant theme of my childhood, in many perspectives, was rehabilitation from my stroke.

When I was five, my family moved to the Washington, D.C. area. Immediately, my mother set out to find a good rehabilitation medicine doctor and physical therapist for me so that I could continue my progress. I also was enrolled in a school which had a program providing physical therapy for physically-disabled students. Furthermore, I went to therapeutic horseback riding one day a week. I had an extremely busy schedule. Nearly every day I had someplace to go in hopes of helping me get better. Unfortunately, none of it was very enjoyable.

Much of my displeasure with having therapy was due to the fact that I didn't understand why I, among all of my peers, was singled out for this. On several occasions, I asked my parents why *I* needed to go to physical therapy, and why *my life* did not more closely resemble the lives of my peers. Yet, my parents' responses invariably went in one ear and out the other.

At my elementary school, which was split between physically-disabled students and able-bodied students, I would look at the students without disabilities, and I would wonder why I couldn't walk like them. When they would go to their after-school activities, I had only physical therapy to which I could look forward. I became angry because I felt different. I just wanted to be like my peers and have a life similar to theirs. There were many times when I found it easier to simply not accept my disability. I would tell myself that nothing was really wrong with me, and that I would get better soon. But, as I realized that this was not true, I just grew increasingly upset. My anger would manifest in resistance to those activities which I did not enjoy but were, of course, ultimately beneficial for me.

I thought more than once about quitting physical therapy. At those times, however, my mother and my physical therapist, Jean Hannah, patiently explained to me the importance of physical therapy in helping me get better. I very much wanted to be able to walk again. And it was the goal of regaining the ability to walk which kept me going through hard times.

Physical therapy primarily consisted of stretching and strengthening exercises which could be very tiring. Luckily for me, Ms. Hannah made the experience of physical therapy as tolerable as possible. Ms. Hannah would work with me for many years. Though in the midst of it all I may not have been having much fun, I now realize how much I benefited from that therapy.

(As I grew older, I moved on to another physical therapist, Susan Ryerson, whose work with me was also very beneficial. I am grateful to all of my physical and occupational therapists for their efforts in helping me.)

In addition to receiving physical therapy, I also was involved in therapeutic horseback riding from an early age. At first, my experience involved lying on my stomach on the horse while the horse walked. My therapist would stretch my muscles, and I also felt the movement of the horse's muscles which was supposed to benefit me. I didn't like being on my stomach because I wanted to conventionally sit in the saddle. It was a strange feeling to not be able to see where the horse was going. Later, I was able to sit in the saddle (although just getting in the saddle was a challenge by itself). Several times, I even lay on my back. I wore a helmet while riding, and there were people on either side of me to make sure that I didn't fall.

(There were a couple of instances, however, when I did fall off the horse. But, when I fell off, I was not deterred, and I just got right back on.)

On those occasions when I was able to sit in the saddle while the horse walked through the nearby woods, I really had fun. It was a form of adventure for me, and I enjoyed those times. Although I realized that the main purpose of my horseback riding was for its therapeutic benefit, I cherished those moments when I could just have fun.

I noticed that after my sessions concluded, my movement was more fluid and not as labored. I continued horseback riding until I was nearly 20.

As if physical therapy and horseback riding didn't keep me busy enough as a child, the rest of my weekday afternoons were devoted to going to Hebrew lessons. My disabilities prevented me (for various reasons) from attending a Jewish Day School or after-school classes at a Synagogue. So, beginning when I was six, I would meet weekly with my Hebrew teacher, Mrs. Reinitz.

Mrs. Reinitz had also taught my father. She never got "old," and she always meant business. First, I learned to read in Hebrew. Later, my studies focused on the Bible. Then, Mrs. Reinitz said it was time to start preparing for my Bar Mitzvah. I started preparing for that day two years in advance. We agreed that, along with reciting certain prayers, I would read a section of the Torah (Five Books of Moses) and chant the Haftorah (a Biblical section from the Prophets). It was a bit more difficult for me to get ready for my Bar Mitzvah than some of my peers because of my learning disabilities. But I practiced...and practiced until I gained command of the words. I never became upset that I had to devote so much time to the preparation because reaching this milestone was very meaningful to me.

Fortunately, Mrs. Reinitz was tremendously committed to seeing me succeed. One time before a lesson, I fell on the sidewalk in front of her apartment. Although I was bleeding from my chin, Mrs. Reinitz insisted that I finish my lesson first. After the lesson was over, my grandfather took me to the hospital for stitches. Mrs. Reinitz had her priorities. In the end, I'm glad she did.

I did well at my Bar Mitzvah. My family was so proud of me. (I was the first boy in my age-group at our Synagogue to become a Bar Mitzvah.) It was a tremendous high point for me. Mrs. Reinitz prepared me so well that I was not even very nervous. My Bar Mitzvah truly showed me firsthand the importance of persistence and determination in achieving one's goals.

Though my life seemed to be dominated by activities to help me gain what most of my peers could take for granted, my parents (and friends) made sure that I could feel like a "normal"

kid as much as possible. Yes, these years were busy, but I also was able to enjoy my childhood.

Beginning when I was very young, my parents instilled in me the belief that my disabilities should not interfere with my enjoying and participating in life, *no matter what.* Having a disability should not get in the way of having fun.

I can't ever recall my parents not letting me try an activity in which I wanted to participate. On the contrary, they always tried to find adaptations so that I could enjoy the activity.

As early as I can remember, I have been interested in sports. Mostly, I have only been able to follow sports. But, on those rare occasions in my childhood when I was able to participate in an athletic activity, it was a wonderful time for me.

At the age of eight (at the time I started to walk again), I really wanted to play sports with my neighborhood friends – especially joining in their games of touch football. They were kind enough to include me, and I was able to play with a few rule changes. I felt so good about being a part of the game, and I had a lot of fun with my friends. I was also able to play baseball with them. Throwing the baseball was relatively easy. Hitting a baseball was somewhat more challenging because I could very easily lose my balance when I swung a bat. I even was able to play a form of basketball with my brother with those small hoops you could put up on a wall. I had so much fun when I could do any activity; I don't ever remember getting tired. I just remember enjoying those moments immensely.

(In more recent years, I have been able to expand my participation in sports. Most notably, advances in adaptive skiing have allowed me to take part in that activity [as I will discuss later]. Also, swimming has provided me with a good way to get exercise. I learned how to swim using only one arm, and I try to swim as much as possible. When I'm in the water, I do not feel as limited by my disability as the water allows me to feel better balanced. I can even walk in the water without any assistance — what a wonderful feeling.)

# CHAPTER 3

Like much of the rest of my childhood, my experiences in school were impacted by my having disabilities.

In first-grade, instead of going to the neighborhood school, I was enrolled in a county school which had a special program for students with physical disabilities. (The rest of the school was for able-bodied students.) I spent my first three years of elementary school at Fair Hill School. I was able to receive physical therapy there — part of which even took place in an indoor pool. Although the program's physical therapy was helpful to me, I found that not all of the teachers were sensitive and understanding to the special needs of the students in the classroom. Some did not seem to appreciate that each of us faced unique challenges and that we would benefit most if we were treated accordingly.

I was fortunate, however, to have several teachers who were very helpful to me. My first-grade teacher, Ms. Ezrol, was very warm and encouraging. I also had a wonderful third-grade teacher — Ms. Shugol. She was in a wheelchair as a result of a horse-back riding accident, and I sensed that she really cared about me.

I particularly recall one experience which greatly benefited me. Occasionally, due to my unsteady balance, I would fall down in class. At first, I didn't believe that I could get up by myself. But Ms. Shugol gently persuaded me to try to do so. It was very difficult, and I initially failed. But Ms. Shugol did not stop giving me encouragement. Finally, after much determination and effort, I succeeded in standing up on my own. I was so pleased to be able to do this. I remain grateful to Ms. Shugol for her invaluable support.

Overall, my most pleasant memories of my years at Fair Hill are of the times when the able-bodied students would participate in activities with the disabled students. For example, our able-bodied peers were introduced to what happens in physical therapy, and they even attempted activities using only one arm. I think these meetings were beneficial to both sets of students. We had a chance to understand each other better. Even as young children, this was very important.

I also have fond recollections from the teachers vs. students basketball game at Fair Hill. I was so happy that I was able to participate in an athletic activity. I played in a wheelchair, and was pushed by a teacher's aide. Even now, I remember how much I enjoyed that day.

A concluding highlight of my time at Fair Hill was when my class took a field trip to the White House. We had juice and cookies, and we were able to meet Mrs. Reagan. The visit was not without a moment of suspense, though. At one point, I lost my balance near a large porcelain vase. My principal was so concerned that I would break the vase. Although I ultimately fell, luckily, I missed the vase.

(One of my main goals at Fair Hill was to make it into a mainstream class — a class for students without disabilities. I found it difficult to be confined to classes with only other disabled students. Seeing the other students' disabilities would sadden me. Moreover, the able-bodied students just seemed to be happier. And I was happier whenever I happened to be around *them*. I never did make it to mainstream classes while at Fair Hill, but I was determined to be there one day — and I would be.)

While I appreciated summers for the break they afforded from school, they offered no respite from physical therapy. In fact, I would often attend specialized intensive courses recommended by my physical therapist.

One course that I will never forget was in the summer after my seventh birthday. My mother took me to the University of Delaware so that I could participate in a six-week course to be held there. Each day, I went to morning and afternoon sessions. I did not really mind the morning session because the main focus was on stretching, which was relatively tolerable. But in the afternoon, I was paired with a therapist — a 6' 3" ex-Marine called "Big Fred." I remember being scared of him. I even recall that I would sometimes cry during sessions with him because he was so demanding of me. However, as I look back on this experience from a distance of 30 years, "Big Fred" helped me in many ways. He was tough, and he pushed me to do more than I thought I could do. My ability to stand and walk today is due in no small part to how hard he worked with me.

To be sure, those six weeks in Delaware certainly were difficult. My mother, brother and I lived in a dorm room. My father was only able to spend time with us on weekends. However, this experience strengthened me both physically and mentally.

And that strength helped me to regain the ability to walk the following year. The first several times I wanted to take a step, I was hesitant to do so for fear of falling. I remember being soaked with sweat. This was partly from physical exertion, and partly from being so scared that my legs would fail to hold me up. I remember sitting back down, and trying to convince myself that I could take a step. Finally, I was successful, and I was so incredibly happy to have reached this milestone.

Physical therapy was generally not very pleasant for me. Yet, it certainly was extremely beneficial in helping me regain function. Further, I learned some valuable lessons from the experience. During those times when I was very discouraged by having to go to physical therapy, I did not quit because I desperately wanted to be able to walk and be independent. And I was able to see that my persistence paid off. Also, I realized that strength and determination could help me overcome great obstacles – for there were many more obstacles that would be standing in my way.

# CHAPTER 4

In the summer after third-grade, I underwent testing which indicated that my stroke had also left me with learning disabilities. Since Fair Hill did not have a program for students with learning disabilities, I transferred to a nearby school that did — Chapel Square.

I enjoyed Chapel Square more than Fair Hill because none of my classmates had physical disabilities. It felt more like a "normal" school.

I was relieved and happy that despite my physical disabilities the community at Chapel Square seemed to accept me. Fortunately, my fourth-grade teacher was very welcoming to me, and she treated me like any other learning-disabled student. In addition to this teacher, there was a kind aide in my class.

That year, I was even asked to deliver the morning announcements for the entire school. The following year, I finally made it into a mainstream class, and I was able to do well.

Unfortunately, Chapel Square closed after my fifth-grade. I transferred to yet another school, Ravensworth, which also had a program for students with learning disabilities. I was also placed in some mainstream classes, and I continued with physical and occupational therapy. The students and staff at Ravensworth made me feel comfortable, and I enjoyed my time there.

With elementary school completed, it was initially unclear which intermediate school I would attend. My neighborhood school, Frost, was multi-storied and was not physically accessible for me. Another nearby school, Holmes, was only one story. Holmes also had a program for students with physical disabilities.

I was disappointed that I could not attend my "home" school, Frost. I had always wished that I could attend the same schools as my neighborhood friends. Yet, I realized the reasons for which Holmes was the better choice for me.

My experience with teachers at Holmes was variable. I recall struggling in a particular mainstream class. Unfortunately, that class's teacher was impatient with me.

On the social side of things, my classmates at Holmes were, fortunately, very welcoming and accepting of me. I do not recall their ever making fun of me. They even made a point to include me in activities. In the annual teachers vs. students basketball game, I was made coach, and it felt very good just to participate. Overall, I have pleasant memories of my time at Holmes.

As eighth-grade concluded, I began to think about the start of high school. I had certain concerns about how I would handle high school. It was the first time that I would be able to go to my "home" school. I was pleased with this development, but I was unsure of how I would even get around the much larger building. I was anxious about whether I would be able to manage the schoolwork, and about whether my classmates would accept me. My excitement for this next step of life was tempered by the awareness that many new challenges were to await me.

# CHAPTER 5

The approach of high school brought with it some anxiety for me, as it does for any student. However, my having disabilities gave me cause for particular concern.

As I entered my teenage years, I realized even more how my disabilities might make it harder for me to fit in with my peers. I was markedly "different," at a time when that was not what I wanted.

Before high school, my parents bought me a motorized scooter which would help me get around the larger school. Though it certainly made life more accessible for me, I soon realized that it would also enhance people's perceptions of me as being "different."

Additionally, though I was glad that I was finally going to my neighborhood school, W.T. Woodson High School, I really didn't know anyone in my class since we had gone to different intermediate schools. I was worried that people would ignore me, or make fun of me. I remember that I was so nervous during my high school orientation. During the first half of my freshman year, I did not feel as if I would ever fit in. It seemed that, no matter what, there always would be a wall preventing me from being "part of the group."

My experience in my Physical Education (PE) class served as an example of the frustration I felt. In PE, I was mainstreamed as opposed to being placed in special classes due to my learning disabilities.   I was happy about this, yet I recall how awful I felt about not being able to participate in any of the activities. I became angry because, now more than ever, I felt like an outsider.

And, during those years, my feeling "different" was affecting my life outside of school, as well.

Fortunately, when I was younger, I was rarely teased or ridiculed because of my disability.   Yet, as I grew older, I became more conscious about how my disabilities would affect how people thought of me.

I began to believe that every time people saw me, they would automatically have a negative opinion of me. I imagined that they would see me as "less than," or that they would make fun of me.

As I entered my teenage years, this type of thinking began to manifest in my reluctance to even go out to the movies, or to a restaurant. I was very concerned with how people would react to me in public. As a teenager, one's appearance means a great deal.  And feeling powerless over how I "appeared" to others led to my feeling poorly about who *I* was.

What may have bothered me the most was my seeming lack of control over this situation.

By deciding not to go out, however, I didn't have to bother worrying about any of this.

Further, as I became ever more cognizant of my disabilities, I had admittedly become increasingly angry and sad.  I am the type of person who does not like being dependent on others. It makes me happier if I am able to do things for myself. Yet, when I would become upset because of my disabilities, I had to push myself to accomplish a certain task. There were occasions when I preferred to wait for others to do for me, even if I might be able to accomplish the particular task. I used to think that because I have a disability, *I deserve to be waited on. Why should I have to help myself? I didn't ask for my disability, so why should I now suffer even more for it?*

Fortunately, with time, I began to change my perspective. I realized how much control I did have in determining, ultimately, who *I* was. Though I could not radically change my outward appearance, I always had control over the internal qualities which defined me — and those aspects which truly represented who I am.

*I also recognized the benefit and strength that comes with overcoming obstacles.* Every time I would help myself instead of looking for help, I would feel better about myself. In fact, I believe that many of my character traits were developed by my perseverance and determination in facing my disabilities.

I therefore saw that I had every reason to feel proud of myself — in good part because of how I chose to face the challenges in my life.

As I realized this, I made a point of going out and experiencing the world. I had strong character, a good personality, and I was intelligent. If people chose just to focus on my disability, then it was going to be their loss. I did not have to fear the opinions of others.

My willingness to open myself up to the world was growing, and my teachers and classmates in high school helped me along in this process.

When I was in tenth-grade, my Physical Education teacher realized that I was very frustrated by not being able to take part in any of the class activities. So, one day he made me a referee for one of the games. I felt good about just participating. I was happy that despite my disabilities I could still feel part of the class. My classmates understood that I, just like them, wanted to feel included. And, I gratefully became aware that they were going to make a point of including me. In return, I began to feel closer to them. I was more willing to talk about my disability. And by talking about it more, *I* actually felt better.

Gradually, I noticed that some of my classmates felt more comfortable engaging with me, and helping me, if needed. It was difficult for me to carry my tray in the cafeteria, so some classmates would accompany me through the line. Others would take turns helping me carry my book bag to the library, where I stored my scooter. At the end of the day, classmates would help me walk to the bus.

As time passed, I felt that fellow students were better able to see *me for who I was* — and not only for my disabilities. My classmates always made sure to keep an eye on me, and help me if I ever needed a hand. But, I didn't get the sense that they felt sorry for me as much as *they saw me as one of their own who happened to have a disability.*

Meanwhile, schoolwork was presenting another set of challenges for me.

Prior to high school, I struggled somewhat academically — especially when I had teachers who were not so sensitive to my learning disabilities. Some teachers did not seem to understand that not all students learn the same way, and had pessimistic outlooks about our capabilities.

Over the years, my biggest challenges in the classroom arose when I had difficulty fully understanding an assignment and had teachers who were not very patient and accommodating when I asked for further explanation. Usually, the issue was not that I was *unable* to do certain things. Rather, the obstacle was more likely that I would need *extra help or guidance* to get things done. Unfortunately, some of my teachers did not seem to understand this distinction.

Those teachers who did acknowledge and appreciate this difference, however, were the most effective. I generally found success in their classrooms. Of course, this trend continued in high school.

Math was always my most feared subject. I often had considerable trouble in comprehending math concepts, and subsequently, I had little confidence in my math skills. Yet, looking back, I think that if I had had better teachers from the start, I likely would have developed more belief in my math abilities, and may have had to struggle somewhat less with the subject.

Reading was also challenging for me. But with the help of good teachers, I greatly improved in this area.

My advice for teachers would be that it is important to remember that all students want to learn and do well. Sometimes, students will need to have things explained more than once or may benefit from hearing alternative explanations. But, that extra time can be extremely rewarding.

Though high school confronted me with different types of challenges, I believe that I made progress every year. By the time I was an upperclassman, I felt very comfortable and had gained more confidence in my abilities. And the highlights of my high school career were to occur at its culmination.

Prior to graduation, I received a letter that I was invited to the annual Awards Night for seniors. I had no idea why I was invited. That evening, I sat through nearly the entire ceremony still unsure of why I was there. Finally, it was announced that the last award of the night was to be given to the graduating student who showed the most courage and determination. It was the Christopher Marshall Award — named in memory of a student who had exemplified these qualities — and its winner was selected by the senior class. It was announced that I had been chosen as that year's recipient of the award. When I went up to the stage to receive this award, the principal gave me a hug, and the senior class stood up and gave me a standing ovation. It was a very special and gratifying moment for me.

Graduation was similarly memorable.

That day, I proudly walked to the stage to receive my diploma. And, though I did not initially notice it, as I was walking back to my seat, my peers gave me another standing ovation. I was again very moved by their gesture. After the ceremony, many of my classmates and teachers congratulated me. I felt so good about what I had achieved.

# CHAPTER 6

Many of my peers likely viewed graduating from high school as an afterthought. For me, though, it was something more. Given my disabilities, there were some people along the way who did not believe that I would get my diploma.

And, for most people, going to college seemed to be out of the question for me. *But, I wanted to push myself further, and I would not be swayed by what other people thought about my potential.*

My parents and counselors recommended to me that starting at a community college would ease the transition to a four-year school. My goal was to get a four-year degree, but I realized that this suggestion made sense in helping me reach my objective.

So, that fall of 1990, I stayed at home and enrolled at the local community college. Some of my classes were challenging, but I luckily had teachers who were patient and kind. I remember that one of my professors allowed me to tape his classes so that I could review the lectures at home. This helped me greatly in learning the material. Though I had been somewhat disappointed by having to start off at community college, I subsequently realized the value of these years in helping to prepare me for what lay ahead.

This period also afforded me an opportunity to achieve an important goal.

When my peers in high school looked forward to getting their driver's licenses, so did I. When I was 16, I passed the written test and got my learner's permit. When it came to operating a car, however, things became a little more challenging — and took a little more time. To drive, I would need special adaptations such as a knob on the steering wheel so that I could steer with one hand. Also, I required a gas pedal that I could control with my left foot. My parents were able to get these adaptations for our car, and I took lessons from an instructor who specialized in helping people with disabilities learn how to drive. We met twice a week. The instructor was sensitive to my disabilities, and thus very patient and effective as a teacher. I took intensive lessons for several months. And it paid off. I was able to pass my driving test on my first attempt.

That same year, I also had to face another, entirely different, test.

Though my heart surgeries when I was a child corrected the initial defect, I have had to have ongoing medical care for my heart's functioning throughout my life.

Before I started at community college, my doctor noticed that my heart rate, at times, was too low. I would need to have a pacemaker installed. I was upset when I initially heard the news because I did not ever hear of a person my age getting a pacemaker. I was worried that something was terribly wrong with my heart. But, after speaking with the doctor, I realized that the pacemaker would just provide an aid to the heart. I was told that my heart, overall, was strong. When I went for my appointment to meet with the surgeon, he inquired if I had any questions. I asked him if I could have the procedure under local anesthesia. I had a concern that my strokes were somehow related to my being on general anesthesia. I knew that this was not necessarily the case, but I still did not wish to receive general anesthesia, if possible. The surgeon understood my concerns, and he agreed to administer only local anesthetics if I were to be able to stay still during the procedure. I was happy with this arrangement, and the procedure was successful.

Though at first concerning, having a pacemaker has fortunately minimally affected my life, and I am grateful for that.

As my second year of community college wound down, I looked forward to moving on to a traditional four-year school. Given my physical and learning disabilities, it was hard to find an appropriate school for me. At a college fair, I learned about the University of Miami, and I made the decision to apply. Soon afterwards, I heard about a program called Threshold at Lesley College in Cambridge, MA. It was a two-year work/study program for people with learning disabilities, and I applied there as well.

I was so excited when I got my acceptance letter from the University of Miami. It felt good to finally be accepted at a four-year school. As it happened, within an hour of receiving the letter, I got a phone call that I had been accepted to the Threshold program. I really wanted to go to Miami. But, unfortunately, its program for students with learning disabilities was not as suitable for me as was Threshold's program.  After a discussion with my parents, it became clear that Threshold would offer me the greater benefit.

It was very difficult for me, at the time, to choose Threshold over Miami. Academic concerns aside, South Florida simply seemed like a more attractive place to live than did New England. However, I understood that attending Threshold made the most sense.

Therefore, I decided to attend the Threshold Program at Lesley College.  Luckily, it turned out that a cousin of mine was already at Lesley; I would know at least one person there even before I got to campus.

I distinctly remember the first day I arrived at Threshold. I quickly became acquainted with my classmates. I also made a point to meet students from the rest of the college because I felt it was important to get to know people from across the campus.

For the first time, I was living away from home. It was initially an unsettling feeling. But I quickly adjusted.  As soon as I started at Threshold, I had a few experiences which helped this process along. In my first week at Threshold, I was on my way to campus in my scooter when I accidentally drove over a nail which punctured a tire.  My Threshold classmates accompanied me back to my dorm, and when I arrived, my wheel was nearly completely flat.  Not knowing what to do exactly, I called AAA.  They helped me to resolve the situation.

Several days after this incident, my scooter broke down while I was off campus. Again, I found a way to get through the situation.  Though initially troubling, these types of occurrences helped me become increasingly confident in my ability to manage any situation.  My sense of independence

— held somewhat in check by my disabilities all of this time — was flourishing.

Later in the year, during a snowstorm, I decided to stay in the center of campus instead of attempting to go back to my dorm in my scooter through the deep snow. However, when I finally did return, my Resident Advisor was very concerned that I was even outside in that weather. But I was not going to let snow impede my independence.

Since Lesley College was small, I became acquainted with a good percentage of the students. In the cafeteria and other gathering places, I would try to get to know as many people as I could. During my first year, I had noticed that some students in the Threshold community were reluctant to integrate socially with the rest of the college. However, I wanted to open myself up to both communities, and I did my best to interact with other Lesley students. In my first year at Threshold, I was the program's representative to Lesley College's student government. I really enjoyed this experience because I was better able to connect with the greater campus community. I even became part of an event-planning committee.

Unfortunately, in my second year, the head of the Threshold program discontinued our representation in Lesley's student government. I was very disappointed because I thought it was important that the Threshold students have opportunities to mingle with students in the greater college. I felt that being able to interact with a wider variety of people was an important part of our experience. I was friends with my fellow Threshold students, but I also appreciated having a link to the other parts of Lesley.

I even participated in field hockey intramurals. Fellow Threshold students and I comprised a team in the college-wide league. The referee put a chair in the goal area so that I could sit down and play goalie. I had fun because I was able to be involved in a team sport. I hadn't been able to do much of that over the course of my life.

Gradually, my Threshold peers also connected more with the rest of the college. During my second year, some Lesley students even came over to the Threshold dorms to socialize. There were two Lesley students with whom I became good friends, and I do wish that there had been a greater overall link between Threshold and the rest of Lesley College.

Our schedules at Threshold were comprised of a split between class and work. My first work placement was at a nursery school, but that only lasted one-half of a year. Unfortunately, due to my physical disabilities, I was very limited in how I could be helpful there. I worked in a nursing home the remainder of my time at Threshold, where I felt I served a more constructive purpose. I delivered mail to the residents and talked with them — providing encouragement, support and company. I enjoyed it because I felt I was able to make some difference by being there.

While at Threshold, I never wavered from my belief that this was but a step toward my goal of getting a bachelor's degree.

In February of my second year at Threshold, I went on a college trip with my family to search for a four-year school that would be a good fit for me. First, we visited a school in central Florida. But, it was small and felt too confining — too similar to Threshold. Then, we traveled to Lynn University in Boca Raton, Florida. I really liked Lynn. The people were friendly and welcoming, and I had a good feeling there during our visit. I applied, and I was accepted.

Admittedly, I had had second thoughts about not going to the University of Miami. I passed up an opportunity to go to a four-year college. Yet, I was patient, and I did what was thought to be best for my long-term future. And now I would have the chance to go to a school that seemed a great choice for me.

With plans set for that autumn, I graduated from the Threshold program in May of 1994. I gave a brief speech from my seat next to the stage in the weekday afternoon ceremony. I remember that the Dean of Lesley College mentioned in her remarks how my positive outlook inspired others — and I remember how good I felt upon hearing those words.

# CHAPTER 7

That fall, I started at Lynn University.

Right from the beginning, I felt at home. Somehow, I don't even remember having much anxiety. I was very excited to attend Lynn because it was one of my dreams to go to a four-year college. I wanted to enhance my education, and I also wanted to have the experience of being at a four-year school. From the beginning, it went smoothly. The students were kind and warm, and the administration was welcoming and accommodating. For example, someone from the cafeteria staff was always available to help carry my tray to the table. The University even solicited my advice on how to make the campus more accessible. I was very impressed with how the school was making a commitment to making me feel comfortable there.

I also felt supported in the classroom. My professors were good, and there were abundant tutoring services available. In fact, over my four years at Lynn, I received several awards for maintaining a high grade-point average. With some of the previous academic difficulties I had encountered, this type of recognition was satisfying.

Socially, the transition to Lynn went fairly well. I quickly began making friends and feeling part of the school community. In my first year, the athletic director asked if I could help out at the scorer's table at basketball games. I was appreciative of his efforts to include me.

It seemed like my first year at Lynn flew by. The week after finals were over, I was already looking forward to my second year. I was very happy with the friendships that I made with fellow students. I felt that the teachers and administrators sincerely cared for me.

My second year went as well as my first. I continued to make new friends and feel more comfortable at the school. I also helped out as a coach of an intramural basketball team.

I truly enjoyed my time at Lynn. I felt connected and accepted within the school, and I also felt that I was a valued friend among my classmates. I believe that people got to know me for who I am, as opposed to just seeing me as "that guy in a scooter."

Of course, not everything was ideal. Initially, there were instances when friends and classmates went out and didn't invite me along because they didn't know if I could physically manage. That was upsetting. There were times when I felt isolated. But, gradually as people realized that I was more physically capable than they thought, they would invite me along to movies or dinner. Being included and accepted was (and is) a great feeling. I'm glad that as people got to know me better, they *did* choose to include me.

Graduation approached quicker than I ever could imagine. My fourth year was the most difficult academically for me. There was one class which was particularly challenging for me. But I had come too far to be discouraged — and I got through the class.

In the spring of 1998, I achieved my goal of receiving a four-year college degree when I graduated from Lynn. It was a day that I had longed dreamed about, and I was so happy that it had finally arrived.

After graduation, I had mixed emotions. My college years were behind me. I was going to miss the students and faculty of whom I had grown fond. It was hard to say goodbye to everyone, but I was very proud of what I had accomplished.

# CHAPTER 8

Attending Lynn had been a great experience for me. I drew a sense of achievement from my four years there, and from finally reaching my goal of getting a bachelor's degree. But I would soon learn that the hard work of getting a job had, of course, just begun.

In my initial search for employment (when the job market was somewhat better than it is currently), I contacted Virginia Rehabilitative Services which acts partly as a job-finding resource for people with disabilities. I made an appointment to see a counselor there. After his evaluation, the counselor told me, "Getting a job will be for you like finding a needle in a haystack." I was hurt by this statement, but I quickly responded that I would find that "needle." I was certainly very discouraged by this meeting. But, with the help of family, I generally managed to stay hopeful and positive.

As time passed, I had a succession of interviews with several organizations. Unfortunately, nothing worked out. I met with a job consultant. She helped me to refine my résumé, and to find prospective employers. However, no success came about, and she ultimately recommended that I go back to Virginia Rehabilitative Services. In the meantime, a family friend asked me to work for him part-time as a receptionist in his Washington office building. I worked there twice a week, and I enjoyed being there. I was treated very well, and I made friends with the other employees in the building. Though I was happy for this opportunity, my goal still remained to find a full-time job.

I subsequently met with another counselor at Virginia Rehabilitative Services who, this time, was very encouraging and helpful to me. I sent more résumés out to prospective employers. Another family friend who worked at the Food and Drug Administration (FDA) also asked me to send her my résumé. She said she would forward it to several people. Soon after, I received a phone call from someone who worked at the FDA who wanted me to come in for an interview. I was very excited that I finally had an interview, and I prepared as much as possible for it. During my interview day, I met with six people. As the day was ending, I met with a seventh person who told me that I was hired. When I heard that, I was very excited and proud. Needless to say, I was eager to start my new job.

Several years after my search began, my first day at a full-time job finally arrived. I was introduced to my co-workers, and they were extremely nice and welcoming. There were some people who worked in my branch who were curious about why I used a scooter. They came into my office to ask me questions about myself, and I explained my disability to them.

My job is as an administrative support clerk. At first, I was assigned small tasks. But once people in the office saw that I was capable of doing more, I was gradually given more to do. I do data entry work and have other responsibilities to make the office run more smoothly. I work with a group of people who are very warm and kind. I know that they are there for me whenever I may need help. I can tell that most of my co-workers do not see me for my disability. Rather, I believe that they see me for my capabilities.

I am very happy to have this opportunity — it really fits with what I wanted in a job. I enjoy what I do, and I enjoy being with my co-workers. This is the type of opportunity I wanted, and I wasn't always sure that I'd be able to find it. I feel like I am doing something constructive, and that I am valued as an important part of the team.

Presently, I am in my seventh year at this job. The road to this point was not always smooth, but the result was certainly worth it.

# CHAPTER 9

As I made the transition into adulthood, though the particular types of challenges presented by my disabilities considerably changed, that did not mean that they were necessarily easier. Now, my concerns centered on whether and how I would be able to live independently and establish a life of my own.

For example, the act of dressing in the morning takes a little more planning and time for me. My job requires business casual attire so I need to wear a dress shirt. Learning how to button my shirt was challenging and took a lot of practice, but I am able to do it independently. I became able to accomplish other tasks related to dressing with the help of occupational therapy and much practice. There are certain things with which I have much difficulty, such as tying shoelaces or fastening pants. However, Velcro has helped in these areas.

Though the microwave is my principal means of food preparation, I am able to get meals for myself. I have unique ways of taking care of household chores, but they get done.

As I have already discussed, I learned how to drive with certain accommodations. My ability to drive enables me to be free of the reliance on others for simply getting around.

Ever since high school, I have mainly relied on a motorized scooter for my mobility. Though I can walk, I can only traverse short distances. My scooter gives me the freedom to go nearly anywhere I want. Especially since I am fortunate enough to have a van that can accommodate my scooter, my disability has become a little less limiting.

Though it may look like fun to some people, using a scooter has its drawbacks. Many doorways or entranceways are too narrow or require turns that are too sharp for my scooter. It is also difficult to get around in crowds of people — many of whom are oblivious to my scooter.

Using a scooter also brings other unique challenges. For example, when people come up from behind me and start talking to me, I sometimes cannot identify the speaker since I cannot easily turn around while seated in my scooter. Thus, I always appreciate when people speak to me when they are in front of me.

Finally, as I have mentioned, it is frustrating that people's main identification of me often is that of "the person who needs to use a scooter." Often, people want to know everything about my scooter before they learn anything about me. I see a scooter as just an object that helps me get from point A to point B. It does not factor into how I view my own identity.

Though I appreciate the freedom my scooter gives me, if my surroundings are not handicapped-accessible, I am stuck. Fortunately, most people do not know what it is like to have a disability. But, that also means that most people do not know what it's like to be unable to do something because of a disability. I am grateful that many things are now accessible in today's society, but truthfully, everything should be.

Unfortunately, there are situations that are still not friendly to those with disabilities. For example, when I am at a sporting event, and the fans suddenly stand up, my view is reduced. I also get upset when I struggle to find accessible seating at any type of event, and later find out that many of the accessible seats are occupied exclusively by able-bodied patrons.

However, many parts of life *have* become more accommodating in recent years for people with disabilities. Through legislation and overall greater sensitivity to the needs of the disabled, I am grateful that accessibility has significantly improved.

These changes have allowed me to be able to take part in activities to which I had long only been a spectator. For example, when I was younger and my family went skiing, I could only sit in the lodge. But over the past few years, I have been able to ski through special programs which allow people with disabilities to ski. I sit on a device which is supported by two skis. I'm not connected to the skis by ski boots. Instead, I'm connected by straps that go around my body. An instructor behind me holds onto me with a rope, and another instructor is present in case I fall. I get up the mountain on a chairlift, like everyone else. (When people see me in a chairlift line, some look amazed that I'm there.) I feel great when I ski because I feel free, and I enjoy the fact that I'm able to be on the slopes just like anyone else. Gradually, I have been able to feel more confident while skiing. When I have fallen, that has only increased my determination to continue skiing. I never feel frightened or discouraged. I'm thrilled to have this opportunity, and I want to get the most out of it. I very much enjoy skiing — and I am always looking forward to taking on new challenges.

Just as the ski slopes have recently opened up for me, I can now better appreciate going to the beach. My scooter is unable to run on the sand, and it is very hard for me to walk on the beach because my crutch always sinks deep into the sand. But, through practice and determination, I have become able to walk on the beach. It is tiring, but it is worth it for the experience. I have also been able to use a special wheelchair which can operate in the sand. This has allowed me to go all the way to the water's edge. It felt wonderful to be able to put my feet in the ocean.

# CHAPTER 10

There are, however, segments of my life which continue to present considerable difficulties for me, and in which I do not feel as if I have made much progress as an adult. These areas include dating, and the realm of building strong social connections.

Often, people appear unsure of how to act around me. My disabilities seem to have transformed me into someone who is very "different." I wish I could tell people that, actually, I'm very much like anyone else. When people use crutches after suffering an injury, we generally do not regard them as altered in other ways.

Though I may appear physically different from most people, that perception of "difference" should not have to carry over to other parts of me. When I meet people, I understand that it may be difficult for them to look past my disability. Sometimes, it seems that there is a sort of shield put up by my disability that prevents people from seeing the rest of me. My disabilities may affect my life, *but I believe that I am much more than my disabilities.*

I am outgoing and I am always interested in meeting new people. Over the course of time, I have been able to make friends both with people who have disabilities, and with those who do not have disabilities.

Yet, as an adult, though I have made friends, being able to establish an active social life has proved difficult for me.

My disabilities present practical difficulties in attending a social event. As I have mentioned, it can be hard to navigate my scooter in the midst of a crowd. Also, when people see me, they seem hesitant to approach me. Part of this likely stems from a discomfort about how to address my disability. However, I'm always glad to talk about my disability. I think that others would be more at ease with me if they knew that they didn't have to be afraid of asking questions about my disability. It should not be the proverbial, "elephant in the room," that everyone notices, but no one speaks about. I hope that when people do take the time to speak with me they realize that I actually may be more similar to them than I am different.

Dating has also been very difficult for me.

Early on, I didn't realize the impact that having a disability was going to make on my dating life. But through various experiences, I began to see how much harder my disability was going to make it to meet someone. When women spend time with me, it generally becomes clear that they just want to be friends.

I have tried online dating. Yet, even women who emphasize the fact that they believe that character is most important lose interest when they realize that I have a disability. I can see how it could be very hard for people to look past my disability. But all I wish for is that people would take the time to see me as an entire person before making a decision about me. I think that when people can see past my disability, they will see a loving, kind, intelligent, easy-going, determined person who has only gained strength by overcoming the obstacles in his life.

I know that dating is hard for everyone, no matter what. While I'm still waiting for a person to see me for who I am, I have faith that this will happen. I believe that there is a person for me, and I will not be discouraged from continuing to search.

# CHAPTER 11

Hopefully, by now I have conveyed my message of how important I believe it is to have a positive outlook in life. Certainly, this thinking has helped me overcome many challenges. Yet, I do not want to conclude this book without disclosing that there have been occasions when I questioned whether I was on the right path, or wondered whether I was fighting a losing battle.

However, these very instances have probably inspired my greatest growth.

There was a time when I thought that if I simply prayed hard enough, my disabilities would disappear. Or, I would hope that if I would just continue to go to physical therapy, my disabilities would substantially diminish. But, as I grew older, I understood that my disabilities, unfortunately, are not going away. They are something with which I must live. This was, and is, a difficult realization to accept. At a certain point, I knew that I faced a choice. I could do my best in confronting life's challenges, or I could quietly withdraw from them, and in so doing, have even a greater reason to feel sorry for myself. Fortunately, I came to the conclusion that avoidance and capitulation, even in the service of self-pity, are of minimal benefit to anyone. Having disabilities is not my fault, nor is it something I asked for. My disabilities should have no role in determining how I think about myself, nor should they limit my enjoyment of life.

Similarly, this book would be incomplete if I did not further discuss the two parts of my life which have helped me maintain a positive outlook in the face of significant adversity — my family and my faith.

Religion has always played an important part in my life. I have always been an Observant Jew. I pray every day and I participate in Synagogue services. I have always maintained faith in G-D. I have never stopped believing that G-D hears my prayers. I did become frustrated when I was younger that all my prayers were not answered immediately, but I have come to believe that G-D does answer my prayers in His Way.

G-D's greatest gift to me has been to surround me with a wonderful family. My parents have truly done everything they could to help me, and they have always been there for me. They, along with my brother, have given me love, support, encouragement and hope for a better future. My father used to tell me that "cannot and will not" are not part of my vocabulary, and I am very grateful for that advice. My family has inspired me to reach for my dreams and have helped me attain my most cherished goals.

My grandparents also were very important to me — inspiring me through their lives and their love for me. I cherish the special relationships I had with all of my grandparents.

# CONCLUSION

*My life has been undoubtedly transformed by my having disabilities. But, I have striven to cope with my disabilities so that my life would not be defined nor limited by disabilities.*

*I believe that having disabilities should not change my life-goals. Though, admittedly, there is much about me which makes me appear different, it does not mean that I expect or want different things from life. Some goals in life may be harder for me to attain. However, this just means that I need to be more determined, persistent and positive. Accordingly, I am a strong believer in the saying, "If there's a will, there's a way."*

*Self-confidence takes us much further in life than does self-pity. One of the secrets in life is in finding out how much more power we have over our lives than we are led to imagine.*

*When people meet me, they sometimes wonder how I keep a positive outlook. Possibly, my attitude is a result of having had to overcome so many challenges in life that I had no choice but to develop reservoirs of resilience and optimism. Or, maybe it stems from life experiences which have instilled in me a deep sense of gratitude for what I do have. Most likely, however, my outlook is a consequence of believing, that while I have certain disabilities in life, I am not disabled. My identity is based on my character and my positive sense of self – entities over which*

*I have control. I am proud of who I am – and nothing can take that away from me.*

*So, have you seen me? Chances are – you have. Because, ultimately, all it really takes is a look in the mirror.*

# Addendum

A Parent's Perspective:

By Myra Gondos

Parenting is difficult, and there is no manual.

Our son, Gary, not yet three years old, had just suffered his second stroke. My husband and I were in a state of shock. Dr. Everett Koop, Surgeon-in-Chief at Children's Hospital in Philadelphia, PA, had just finished making his evening rounds. He stopped by Gary's bed and we talked. He was such a warm and kind man, so I asked him, "What do we do next?"

Dr. Koop softly replied, "Take him home and show him how to enjoy life." He was the only doctor who gave us positive advice. (A few years later, Dr. Koop went on to become Surgeon General of the United States. He was a wonderful choice for that position.)

We took Dr. Koop's words to heart and tried our best to adhere to them. Just earlier that day, one of the staff cardiologists recommended that we discuss possible institutionalization for Gary. I told him, "Never!" and walked away. Unfortunately, a prevalent feeling among doctors in the '70s was that if there were a "serious problem," institutionalization was the answer. We knew the situation was very difficult, but Gary was coming home with us.

Pregnancy and delivery had been normal. When Gary was one month old, he was diagnosed with a heart murmur. But Gary seemed to be doing well until he reached five months. Then, he started to have trouble keeping food down. Subsequently, during a routine examination, Gary's pediatrician said that Gary was in heart failure. I was stunned. The pediatrician then proceeded to prepare to give Gary the inoculations that were originally scheduled as part of the visit. I protested vehemently against this as Gary had always had a reaction to these shots. Yet, the doctor insisted and jabbed them into Gary anyway.

We immediately brought Gary to Georgetown Hospital in Washington, DC where it was determined that he had a serious heart defect. After Gary underwent cardiac catheterization to diagnose the cause of his heart failure, we were sent directly to Children's Hospital in Philadelphia for an intervention that was quite new at the time. Gary had a condition called Total Anomalous Pulmonary Venous Return. In layman's terms, Gary's heart was not pumping oxygenated blood to his body. The surgeons decided to put a hole in Gary's heart, following a new procedure developed by Dr. William Rashkind. It would allow Gary to survive for several years until he could have a second, more invasive surgery — one that could ultimately "repair" the defect. Dr. Rashkind performed this temporizing procedure successfully. When Gary woke up, however, we startlingly realized that he could not move the right side of his body — and had likely had a stroke. We asked, "What happened?" The medical staff simply replied, "Sometimes these things happen after surgery."

I never thought that infants could have strokes, but our child had just suffered one. "How could something like this happen to such a young child and why?" I asked, despairingly aware that even if I were given an answer, I would not be consoled. After a week, we were told we could take Gary home. Our little baby was partially paralyzed and had a serious heart problem. We were heartbroken, and so were our families.

My husband, Gordon, was 27, and had just finished the first year of his psychiatry internship. I was 24. Gordon had studied medicine, child development and psychology during his training. I am a speech therapist. We were certainly aware of the many problems that can affect a baby. When illness strikes one's own child, however, all book learning is forgotten. Instead, fear and helplessness take over. We understood what happened physiologically, but as to, "Why?"...that question has never ceased to haunt us.

However, we knew that our total focus must be on helping Gary get better. Natural instincts of loving and caring are most important. Our most valuable guidance came from our parents. All four of Gary's grandparents gave us so much strength and support in our efforts to help Gary.

When Gary was five-and-a-half months old, physical therapy began. Most therapists in outpatient settings had never treated such a young baby. We found a wonderful young therapist at the local hospital who was willing to work with Gary. Thus, we began a daily routine of physical therapy that seemed to last forever.

My background as a speech therapist taught me the importance of aggressive intervention and stimulation in such situations. Yet, I was also keenly aware of all the other problems which could develop. Since we were living in Newport News, VA, where my husband was stationed as an Army physician, we were quite far from a large teaching hospital.

I knew I could not afford to squander any time dwelling on all of the possible negative sequelae resulting from the stroke. Rather, I had to constructively focus my thoughts on how I could help Gary. I took out my books on Child Development and devised my own infant stimulation program. "Focus on the positive," I kept repeating to myself.

Days were spent with physical therapy, speech and language stimulation, along with the other routines involving a fairly young child. But I never could forget that, fundamentally, Gary's needs were like those of any other infant — just much more intensive.

By the time Gary was two-and-a-half years old, he had started walking, albeit with a limp, and he was relatively independent. He was always a happy child and certainly received much attention. We had moved back to Albany, NY in June of 1973 where my husband continued his residency following his two years in the Army. Once in Albany, physical therapy was increased to twice a day, every day. We essentially lived in the hospital. We were there by 10:00 AM, and returned home by 4:00 PM. As the youngest child in the Rehab Center, it was as if all the people there were his extended family.

Two very special people helped care for Gary. He had a fantastic physical therapist, Mrs. VandeBogart, as well as a wonderful physiatrist, Dr. Kress. They both showered Gary with much love and encouragement. Therapy was very intensive, and successful. In the days leading up to his second surgery, Gary was already running, talking and generally being just like a regular two-year-old. He was inquisitive, curious and very endearing.

In March 1974, life changed once again. The surgery to permanently resolve the heart defect was successful, but to everyone's disbelief, Gary had had another stroke. This time, the stroke was bilateral. *How resilient could a child possibly be*? Gary had to learn to swallow again, to sit up again, to speak again, and to hopefully walk again.

There was no time to waste with anger or depression. We already knew that we had to provide intensive therapies in order to help Gary regain movement, speech and the other functions lost due to the stroke. Prior to the surgery, as I had mentioned, Gary was running, talking and full of energy. Now, he could not even sit up alone. He could not talk. He could not feed himself.

At first, the Cardiology Team denied that Gary had a stroke. Instead, they simply called it psychological depression. *If only that had been true.* We immediately knew that Gary had suffered another stroke. We saw his frustration over being unable to speak or to even feed himself. But the doctors insisted that he was just depressed. Finally, a neurologist confirmed our worst fears. Gary had indeed suffered another cerebral hemorrhage which caused extensive neurological damage.

As a child of Survivors of the Holocaust, I asked my father how he and my mother were able to go on after having experienced so much heartbreak — including losing their first child at

Auschwitz along with so many members of their families. My father told me that he prayed for the strength and wisdom to do what had to be done to resume their lives, and to move on. And, somehow, my parents were able to move on. Using their example and inspiration, *we were able to move on*, focusing on Gary's recovery, but never forgetting Dr. Koop's advice to "show him how to enjoy life." We wanted Gary to participate in the same activities as did his able-bodied peers. There were play groups, and nursery school. Although Gary was the only child with a physical disability, the teachers were willing to accommodate. Inclusion is much easier when children are younger.

Gary thrived and improved. When Gary was five years old, we moved to Virginia. We welcomed the arrival of our new son, Brian, a month after our move. Gary had long asked for a brother, and we were so grateful to be blessed with another son. Despite their five-year age difference, they have always been very close.

Now, a whole new chapter was beginning. School was to start — where should Gary go? We tried public school kindergarten. We were instructed to enroll Gary in a special program for physically-disabled students. Unfortunately, very little therapy was actually provided.

So, the search started again. Gary attended the Child Development Center which was a fair distance from our home. At least, Gary would receive therapy there every day. As a newborn, Brian learned to travel a lot.

When Gary was to begin first-grade, we dealt with the same issue of determining which school would be the best for Gary. There were no private programs from which to choose.

Fortunately, Special Education in our home county of Fairfax County, VA was highly regarded.

Gary's left side gradually regained strength following his second stroke, but his right side remained very much affected. Gary needed occupational, physical and speech therapy.   I knew that I had to do my homework. And that started with learning to become an advocate.  With the new laws in force, every child with a disability was entitled to an Individual Education Plan (IEP). Luckily, I found a class teaching parents how to most effectively advocate for the best interests for their children.

That class at The Parent Educational Advocacy Training Center was invaluable.  This was the Center's first course in Fairfax County. The manual was huge; there was a tremendous amount of information to absorb.  I learned how to work with the school.  By the time of our first IEP, the school and I were able to formulate a plan for Gary.  I did not want it to be "us" against "them."  I knew that the school truly wanted the best for the students.  But, I also knew that they had to deal with other considerations.

The most significant of these considerations is, of course, money.  Therapy is expensive.  Gary attended Fair Hill Elementary School which had recently undergone a renovation whose projects included an indoor pool.  The only problem was that the pool was not used because no one could be hired (because of the lack of financial resources) to help the children dress after a session.  This called for quick action.  I organized other parents, and we went before a task force at the county level.  We asked that, either there be more funding so that the pool could be used during the week, or that parents be allowed to use the pool on weekends with their children.  Both ideas were vetoed.  So, I organized a group of mothers, and we were there on most school days to help the children so that they could receive therapy in the pool.

By working closely with each other, we (our group of mothers) realized that we had established a wonderful support group. In those days there were no support groups for parents as there are now. We went on to establish the first parents' advocacy group in Fairfax County for children with physical disabilities. We found strength in numbers. Soon, we would approach Fairfax County's Recreation Center and request that they put together an adaptive aquatics program for our children. That was the birth of an extremely successful program that has since grown tremendously. *Advocacy is the key.*

We urged a swimming instructor from the Red Cross to try a class with our children. The children loved the class, and the instructor realized that this experience was not so different from teaching non-disabled children. She would just need more volunteers. That would not be a problem.

Gary gradually regained more function during these years. With the support of our private physical therapist, I insisted that Gary not use a wheelchair to get around school. I wanted him to walk on his own — which he could do with the aid of a walker. I was so afraid of his muscles atrophying. I did not want him to lose everything he had gained from the previous physical therapies.

Then, of course, there was the academic component of school. I was aware that Gary suffered from visual-perceptual and language disabilities as a result of his stroke. Yet, it almost seemed as if his teachers did not want to tell me that Gary had learning disabilities, for fear of upsetting me. I begged the school to test Gary for learning disabilities. At that time, public education for children with disabilities was a hot topic with a new law in place (PL 94-142). Parents could have an even more significant say in the education of their children.

Often, parents are in denial of a serious issue. *I just told the school that we simply wanted whatever was available to help our son.* Looking the other way would not help anyone. Gary would need interventions for his learning disabilities as well as the services for his physical disabilities.

Unfortunately, the amount of physical therapy Gary received at school was still not enough, so we continued privately. That was a bone of contention with the school, but they could not stop us from wanting to provide help for Gary. We also began therapeutic horseback riding, which was so beneficial. There, too, extra hands were needed. My work with therapy started to rapidly expand. It was good that I was young, and able to do it all.

We were lucky to find a wonderful physical/occupational therapist, Jean Hannah, who worked with Gary, and was able to help Gary progress as much as possible. Summers were spent in intensive sessions where Gary received hours of NeuroDevelopmental Treatment (NDT).

We even spent one summer at the University of Delaware attending an NDT training class for therapists. NDT was becoming regarded by many as the most effective method to help children with physical disabilities stemming from Cerebral Palsy, or from a stroke. NDT was based on the Bobath method developed in England. The idea was to follow the pathways of development that an infant normally goes through, and to try to put the affected child through all of these pathways.

That summer, young therapists honed their newly acquired skills in NDT on children who were brought by parents hoping for any improvement. At the time, Gary was seven, Brian was almost two, and we were living in a dorm. Conditions were not ideal, but we could see that this therapy was working. Gary's therapist was a former Marine, named "Big Fred." He was tough, but he helped Gary immensely. Gary was worked so hard that he occasionally was in tears. But it paid off. By the end of the summer, he was able to walk again — now, unassisted.

The head of the NDT program was Dr. Christine Nelson. She practiced and taught NDT as a pediatric therapist in Maryland. She then moved to Cuernavaca, Mexico to set up a clinic there. In the years following our summer in Delaware, Gary's muscles had tightened up following growth spurts (a recurring problem). So, in March 1980, we headed off to Dr Nelson's clinic in Mexico for two weeks of intensive therapy. This was not a luxury vacation, but it was more valuable than any vacation could be. Gary came home walking again. We always kept telling him he's tough. *He was, and is.*

Unfortunately, so much of Gary's life was devoted to overcoming the injuries caused by his strokes. Yet, we have always striven to be faithful to Dr. Koop's wise words. We could not just cover Gary in bubble wrap and protect him. Gary wanted to learn how to ski. He was able to take lessons at age twelve and loved it. More recent advances in adaptive skiing have enabled Gary to increase his participation in the sport. Swimming and horseback riding are other activities in which Gary is able to take part.

Most important, Gary gained the gift of mobility with a small motorized scooter. When Gary was to enter high school, we knew that he would not be able to walk between classes (his walking was limited to short distances). We were able to get him a motorized scooter. Subsequently, we have been able to purchase adapted vans so that we could transport the scooter.

Luckily, modern technology has helped break down so many barriers to independence.

Schools changed, offices moved, but throughout Gary's childhood, the routine largely remained the same. School followed by therapy comprised the daily routine.

In addition, we felt that private tutoring would be helpful as an intervention for Gary's learning disabilities. Although my training could have helped me to serve in this role, it was better to have someone else, other than Mom, help. Gary was aided by a tutor for quite a few years, and it certainly was worth the extra time, cost and effort. While Gary had many wonderful teachers, he also had some teachers who were seemingly insensitive to his learning disabilities. Tutors were valuable resources in these situations.

Overall, life was marked by setbacks and minor breakthroughs; it always seemed like a roller coaster ride. Throughout, Gary handled everything with strength, confidence, and an unwavering positive outlook. No matter the circumstance, Gary made the most of any experience.

An example of this was Gary's experience in becoming a Bar Mitzvah. Gary wanted to do what was expected of any Bar Mitzvah. He had the most wonderful private tutor, Mrs. Rachel Reinitz, who also had prepared Gary's father for his Bar Mitzvah. Gary started to study two years prior to his Bar

Mitzvah date. He had lessons every week and was determined to do it all. When Gary's Bar Mitzvah day finally arrived, he was terrific. There were no dry eyes in the sanctuary.

Whether it was learning to walk, preparing for his Bar Mitzvah or working on a school activity, Gary set his goals, and then followed through. We were there to support, but the determination had to come from him. As parents, that was an important lesson for us to learn. He wanted to show that he could accomplish those goals.

And then, seemingly in a flash, childhood had passed and Gary was ready for life's next stage.

The lessons that I learned along the way are many. Love, nurturance, and caring are vital to all children. Those all come first. Gary's needs essentially were the same as those of any other child. The extra therapies and interventions were just included in the whole package.

In addition, keeping on top of the newer therapies and the advances in knowledge is essential to being able to help one's child as much as possible. Also, I saw that what may work for one child may not be what's best for another. One must always keep in mind the individuality of each child, and work towards his/her best interest. Parents should always remember that it's not about their own egos. We should love our child for who he/she is and help our child develop his/her full potential. It is critical that a child have good self-esteem. The worth of the adage, "Emphasize the positive," simply cannot be overstated. Children thrive on being loved and accepted, and it is so important that each child feel good about his/her identity.

Transitions are always a difficult time. At the end of high school, we wondered about Gary's next step. Gary was determined to go to college. We decided that it might be best if Gary were to start out at our local community college. From there, Gary went on to a program at Lesley College in Cambridge, MA, called Threshold.

At Threshold, students with learning disabilities are able to attend classes and receive work experience. After two years, students graduate with a certificate. Gary was the only student with a physical disability at Threshold. After he was accepted, the school realized that not every part of campus was accessible for his scooter. Cambridge is an older city and many of its streets did not have curb-cuts. The school asked us to accompany Gary all over campus to troubleshoot the difficult areas. The city of Cambridge was very accommodating and made changes to some sidewalks and streets. (Of course, having the Americans with Disabilities Act [ADA] in place was considerably helpful in getting this done.)

Although Gary had never lived away from home before, Gary handled this transition very well. No matter the situation, Gary confidently persevered. Threshold's administration and staff may have been even more protective over Gary than I was. Gary managed to get around in snow and ice, and would show up to class, no matter the weather. Although there were times when he even had to share the road with cars, Gary remained undaunted. Gary was so determined to pursue higher education and get a college degree. Threshold was a wonderful program and experience for Gary.

After finishing at Lesley, Gary entered Lynn University in Boca Raton, FL. He certainly welcomed the change in climate. At Lynn, Gary completed a four-year college curriculum. People wondered how we could let him go to school that far away. You have to believe in your own child. As parents, we know our kids the best. We always felt that if he were able to do it, we should not stand in the way because of our own concerns. Everyone should be able to have the freedom of being independent. And, we were only a two-hour flight away. As he did at Threshold, Gary managed extremely well at Lynn.

Yet, there was one instance when the two hours that separated us seemed interminable. Gary became very sick as he was about to travel home for summer break following his first year at Lynn. I could hear it in his voice. I immediately got onto a flight so that I was able to meet Gary in Atlanta, where he was changing planes. I'm very glad that I went. Gary was so weak that he could not even get out of his airplane seat without help. He had a terrible case of pneumonia, and it took weeks for him to recover.

Gary graduated from Lynn in 1998 and we were thrilled for him. He was determined to get his degree and he did. He accomplished another milestone in his journey.

With diploma in hand, Gary began to look for a job. Employment of people with disabilities presents many challenges. Gary sent out résumés, attended job fairs, and worked with the local Department of Rehabilitative Services. This was all to no avail. Finally, a good friend of ours gave him a job as a receptionist in his office. Gary loved the position as he is truly a "people person." Unfortunately, the job was interrupted by the events of 9/11. The requirements of the position changed due to the need for enhanced security measures.

The job search began again. Fortunately, Gary already had a Schedule "A" certificate which would hopefully help him find a Federal Government job for a person with disabilities. A wonderful friend suggested he send a résumé to the Food and Drug Administration; Gary has been successfully working there for seven years. Gary has enjoyed his time there, and has made many friends. His co-workers have also gotten to know him for *who he is,* which is especially gratifying.

Further, Gary has taken on the responsibility of living in his own apartment, paying his bills and being ever more independent.

Gary has always adapted to each stage of life with maturity and confidence. To be sure, adulthood, like all previous stages, has presented its own set of tests.

Social inclusion has become a greater challenge for Gary as he has gotten older. During elementary school and high school, Gary made friends with the children in our neighborhood and with the children of our friends. The hardest period to negotiate is adulthood. Parents can no longer help provide the social networks, and young adults do not accept their disabled peers as readily as they do when they are children. There is still much work to be done in educating the public about people who have disabilities. Perhaps, upon meeting people with disabilities, people are uncomfortable asking, "What happened?" or have difficulty relating to those with disabilities. But, Gary's wish to be accepted by others is not any different from that of anyone else. Barriers are coming down, but too slowly. *There is still much work to be done.* Gary has a positive identity, and therefore cannot understand why others see him so differently. Gary simply hopes to be accepted for who he is. At the least, he just wishes not to be ignored. We, as a society, need to do a better job of looking beneath the surface to see the real person.

Being a parent is not easy; we always hope and pray that we are doing the right thing. With each child there may be unique challenges. But if we are guided by love and by our children's best interests, I believe that we will always be on the right path.